IRELAND: PRESENCES

IRELAND:

PRESENCES

DANIEL KAUFMAN
Introduction by Pete Hamill

ST. MARTIN'S PRESS, NEW YORK

Book Design By Deborah Daly

Published 1980 in the United States by St. Martin's Press, Inc., 175 Fifth Avenue, New York, New York, 10010

Printed and bound in Hong Kong
by South China Printing Co.

Library of Congress Cataloging in Publication Data

Kaufman, Daniel.
    Ireland presences.

    1. Ireland—Description and travel—1951–
—Views. 2. Northern Ireland—Description and travel—
Views. I. Title.
DA982.K38   914.15082'3   80-11658
ISBN 0-312-43591-6

For David Viscott
who Helps to See

For the opportunity to spend a year in Ireland photographing without restrictions, I am grateful to the Fulbright-Hays Fellowship Foundation, and also to the Scholarship Exchange Board of Dublin, Ireland, which administered the Grant.

contents

INTRODUCTION

It is difficult now for me to go back to Ireland. Yes: there are moments when I am exhausted by the angular passions of American cities and long for green fields and soft rain, the stillness of market towns on summer afternoons, the music of a language spoken without hardness, and evenings under immense and changing skies. I yearn for connection to the land of the Celtic past, that time of druids, bards, artisans, and magic, in a world that was still empty. I want to combine with Irish history, with the places and tales that were passed to me by my parents before they too joined the never-ending Irish diaspora. I want the details of the present: the smell of wet wool in steamy winter pubs, cut glass, polished wood, peat fires, dark creamy pints of Guinness, a burst of sudden laughter, the red cheeks of children, the sound of a tin whistle, the smell of old books in the stores beside the Liffey, bells, dogs in fields, bacon at breakfast, the clear eyes of old women, and ballads in the rainy night:—ballads and fiddles; mouth organs and ballads:—and their plaints, shouts, whispers, their defiance, their resentments, their unforgiving memory.

But usually when the yearning hits, on some vertical New York street or some sun-blanched sandy hill in California, I don't choose to go to Ireland. I don't head for an airport, to be locked in some winged steel cannister and hurled across the Atlantic. I've lived too much in Ireland, in Dublin and Belfast and Derry, in the years since 1962. And now, for me, Ireland is too full of hurt. I do not want to be a tourist in other people's pain. It is much easier to make the journey in the pages of this book.

The hurt comes from the past, of course, and is carried into the present as part of the cargo of old crimes. The Irish, like the Jews or the Armenians, are a people To Whom Things Were Done. They did not launch armies against other nations; their fleets did not land on foreign shores. They were a people warred against, a people invaded, a nation shredded by the iron will of others.

And so today, a foreign visitor sees an ancient tower on the Cliffs of Moher, in County Clare, and freezes it with his Nikon; some Irishmen see another picture: blood, flames, iron-clad infantry, bowmen on the hills, catapults and arrows, and the lances of dragoons, followed by the destruction of families, the murder of a splendid language wielded by shepherds and poets alike. The visitor listens to the blarney of the tour guide, the shamrocking of history, the weaving of gossamer inventions; some Irishmen hear the dark murmur of an antique past, when the Irish learned to lie in order to live, convincing the English tax collectors that a cow was a rabbit, disguising feeling, using charm and double-talk to live another hour. The men and women who deal with tourists are decent and skillful and take delight in the performance, but they have the skills of actors, and those skills were fashioned to protect a people against a crime.

That is why there are faces in this book that seem to be hundreds of years old. Walk into the Bogside in Derry. A child comes around the corner. He is ten years old, fresh-faced, hair trimmed neatly, cheeks rouged by hearth fires; but his eyes are as old as tombs. The faces, the places, the people of Ireland have been shaped by the dark past. You think you have come to know an Irishman, and then there is one more surprise, one fur-ther revelation, one shard of memory, one buried resentment, that alters everything.

* * *

Look at these faces, and try to imagine their pagan past, when Ireland was a communist society, led by kings—a country without cities, whose people believed in an after-life, but not in sin or punishment. They were makers of beautiful objects, wrought from the gold of the Wicklow mountains: bracelets, rings, torques, brooches, golden collars. And they were from the beginning a mixed people: Picts, then Celts or Gaels in the sixth century B.C., and later the Norse and the Danes, warriors and plunderers, but the makers of cities: of Dublin and Cork and Waterford. The island was covered then with forests, in the distant centuries before the English denuded the hills, feeding the fires of their homes or building the English fleets. For centuries, before the English, there was no written language, and the tale of the people was carried in the heads of the druids. In the Heroic Age, when even Julius Caesar decided it was not worth battling the wild men of Ireland, kings ruled small groups of the Irish, but the power of those kings was severely limited. There was, for example, no central government, and individual kings could not pass judgment on those they led; justice was a function reserved for druids, who were carefully trained for the task. Kings could not appoint successors, and the crown did not automatically pass to the king's oldest son. Instead, candidates would be drawn from a wide choice of relatives and the new king elected from that group, often before the death of the reigning king to avoid quarrels. Communal life revolved about cattle, but there was ample room for music, and for stories, at the great cattle fairs and the meetings of tribes, at which there were also dances and sporting contests and horse races. The communal life of the Celts was not feudal or oppressive. From all accounts, it was basically just.

Then came St. Patrick. He was first brought to Ireland as a slave, captured at fifteen by Irish seacoast raiders from some Roman settlement on the coast of England. Most accounts say that he was a swineherd in Ireland for almost six years (probably in County Mayo), escaped, returned to England, became a Christian and then a priest, and was told in a dream that he should return someday to Ireland and convert the heathen Irish. So he did, in about A.D. 425, and he must have been a remarkable man, because by the time of his death in 460, his triumph was almost total.

The Christian sect flourished in the damp Irish countryside and permanently entered the Irish soul. Men and women who once saw gods in the rivers and streams, the hills, the valleys, and the sea now swore allegiance to an imported monolithic god, one who could not be seen until death. He was a cruel god, a vengeful god, a god conceived by men who lived in deserts, and for the first time the notion of sin appeared in Irish life, along with its corollary, punishment. Irish Christian scholars retreated into monasticism. Generation would flow into generation, old places fall into ruin, the earth thicken with blood and then dry before the new spring, but the idea of sin would endure.

"We were experts on Sin: original sin, venial sin, mortal sin, sins of omission and commission, occasions of sin," wrote Irish novelist James Plunkett in 1972. "There were reserved sins too, but these were for some obscure villainies. We were taught how to dissect sin in an examination of conscience; the gravity of the sin, its frequency, the amount of pleasure taken in it, was it deliberate or involuntary, had you gone into the occasion of sin. We were all little anatomists, trained to subject sin and its by-products to endless analysis. When all was parsed and analyzed and ready for inspection, the slide clicked open and the soul was laid bare. Then the priest gave absolution. His hands held the keys to heaven and hell."

The priests of the Christian god swiftly replaced the druids, and it was no accident that the Irish, over the ensuing centuries, became obsessed with death. That was the moment when all would be settled, when piety would be rewarded and license punished, when all the years of self-denial would be transformed into eternal glory, or unredeemed sins lead to the flames. Life could be seen as a mere first act, not complete in itself until death had raised the curtain for the second, and final, act. It was a splendid notion to sell to people who lived on an island, cut off for long years from the rest of the world; if there could be no true happiness until death, then a hard struggling life was man's lot. The priests, and all those secular agencies that derived their power from priestly authority, used this ghastly notion to enrich themselves while impoverishing the Irish. The most devastating revolutionary slogan I ever saw was also the most Irish. It was painted on the wall of a cemetery on the Whiterock Road, and said, very simply: IS THERE A LIFE BEFORE DEATH?

Christianity also paved the way for the Christian English, who came to hurt and conquer. First the Church undermined the Celtic social system, and then, as the Church came under the direct sway of Rome and centralized authority, it authorized the introduction of the hateful feudal system and opened the doors to the Anglo-Norman invaders. Five centuries after Patrick, the country had become nominally Christian, but the people had not truly changed their ways. A typical complaint about his fellow Irishmen was addressed by Maelmaedoc O Morgair (born in 1095) to his abbot. Speaking of himself in the third person, he described a missionary journey he had made around Ireland:

"He discovered it was not to men but to beasts he had been sent; in all the barbarism which he had yet encountered, he had never met such a people so profligate in their morals, so uncouth in their ceremonies, so impious in faith, so barbarous in laws, so rebellious to discipline, so filthy in life, Christian in name but pagans in reality."

Maelmaedoc was apparently a great organizer who divided the country into thirty-six basic dioceses, with central authority in Armagh. He traveled at least twice to Rome, and it could have been his urging (along with that of other members of the Irish hierarchy) that in 1154 led Pope Adrian IV to grant Henry II of England the right to invade Ireland and "enlarge the bounds of the Church, to teach the truth of Christian faith to the ignorant and rude, and to extirpate the roots of vice from the field of the Lord." Certainly, in the events that were to follow, the Church offered no resistance.

Adrian was the first and last English pope, and part of the deal called for Henry to make cash payments to the pope's treasury from the expected looting of Ireland. But Henry was too busy consolidating his empire

(it then included England, Normandy, Anjou, Poitou, and Aquitaine in France) and did not immediately take action. Indeed, the Irish themselves were to produce their own betrayal. The villain was a man named Dermot MacMurrough of Leinster, who had suported Murtough Mac Lochlainn in a contest for supreme king of Ireland (*Ard Ri*) against Rory O'Conor of Connacht. O'Conor won the struggle and MacMurrough left Ireland in August 1166 as a loser. But he had not given up on Ireland. He went to England, planning a devastating return. His immediate goal was to win back his own provincial chieftainship. He tried to interest Henry II in an alliance and failed. He then made an arrangement with a man named Richard FitzGilbert deClare, Earl of Pembroke, known forever after in Irish history as Strongbow. MacMurrough promised Strongbow the right to succeed to the chieftainship of Leinster (one of the four Irish provinces) and threw in his daughter Eva as a wife. Strongbow raised a small army of Normans, Welsh, and Flemings for MacMurrough, who went back to Ireland in 1167.

MacMurrough and his men were beaten back by the Irish under O'Conor. But they were not finished. MacMurrough bargained and talked and waited for Strongbow, who was recruiting a larger army in Wales. Strongbow arrived in 1169, with the tacit approval of Henry II. Dublin fell on September 21, 1170. When MacMurrough died suddenly, Strongbow claimed the "kingship" of Leinster, but even the clans of Leinster revolted at this. Soon Strongbow was fighting all over Ireland, against various Irish clans and against the Dano-Irish king of Dublin and his Norse-Irish army. Strongbow sent an urgent message to Henry II, dealing him into the Irish war and offering him everything he had conquered. Henry II landed in October

1171 with 500 knights and 4,000 men at arms, and the conquest of Ireland by England had begun.

* * *

Today Ireland reeks with history. The centuries that passed were sporadically bloody, as the Irish continued to resist. It would take five centuries before the old Irish language and culture were completely broken by some of the most steadily ruthless assaults of one nation against another in European history. Today, in the streets of Belfast and Derry, there are brave men and women fighting to break the last vestiges of the old illegal domination. They have been dismissed by some as murderous thugs, by others as romantic fools, but they possess their history. They can speak of Strongbow and what followed: feudalism, the betrayals of the Church, Cromwell, the Boyne, the Flight of the Earls, the Plantation of Ulster, the horrors of the Great Famine when Englishmen ate the meat of Ireland and a million people died, Wolfe Tone, O'Connell and Parnell, and Easter 1916. The men and women of the Provisional IRA are fueled by memory, but this is not a political book. It is not about them. It is not specifically about history, except insofar as the fog and drizzle and wild beauty of the land explain the love of country that has led so many brave and foolish human beings to die for that small tragic nation.

I wish I could go there now as an ordinary citizen, not charged with reporting the fighting in the North, free of confusion over alliances and responsibilities. But I can't. As I write, men and women are dying in the final phase of an old quarrel. I might visit Ireland as a reporter, but not as a child of the Irish diaspora. Not now. Not until the Irish flag billows in the breeze over Derry and Belfast, Newry and Strabane. Until then, there is this book, with its beauty and its ghosts.

Pete Hamill
New York, 1979

PHOTOGRAPHER'S FOREWORD

I came upon presences everywhere in Ireland: a lone tree that had the aura of a being alive with untold stories; bluebells in a woods that made me hold my breath lest I disturb their silence; two white horses in a field, staring into my camera; stones on a wet hillside that stood together like lost souls; sheep in the sunset with halos I craved to touch but could only photograph.

Presences stopped me short on dirt roads, in back alleys, on mountain tops, and along the city streets. Accidental arrangements of form and color amazed me in the most unlikely places. I was often startled by the power of ordinary things—a telephone booth, a red door, a store front.

Along the grayest of Dublin's streets a bright fruit stand appeared like magic (Plate #4). Children played around it and the misty light seeped into the scene from everywhere.

The photographs are frozen memories of my experience. Sometimes it is nearly impossible to believe the orderliness and beauty of things—a ballet of trees at dusk, a flock of sheep moving together in perfect convergence toward the ocean. Each picture is made from some kind of inner necessity. There is always an urgency to record something extraordinary before it isn't there to see anymore.

Aqueous light pervades a misty sea cliff. The feeling I get in my stomach compels me to photograph. The light makes me clench my teeth in excitement. I often find myself squinting, as if to soften the intensity of the experience.

Ideally, I make pictures only when I cannot resist. A photograph is seldom if ever consciously planned. Pictures take me. Contrivances are usually failures. Sometimes I will wait for hours for the color of the sky to change or hold my breath until the right silhouette appears. But I try not to waste time struggling to make a photograph out of elements that do not come quickly together on their own.

The process of making a photograph involves contact on both a personal and a universal level. When I took the picture of the shepherd on a hill near Dublin, it was Christmas Day (Plate #18). I was three thousand miles from home and felt terribly lonely; I experienced an intense feeling of relief when I saw the dogs and the man alone on the hill. This is the picture from Ireland that gives me the most pleasure. I felt as though I had been *given* the picture, for reasons I do not fully understand.

At the time of this picture I was open and vulnerable. This is when I am able to make the most satisfying photographs. It is fascinating that people seem to connect with these images on an emotional level. I am learning that the heart sees more than the eyes, and more than the mind can understand.

Daniel Kaufman
Wellesley, Massachusetts
August, 1979

A NOTE ON TRAVEL PHOTOGRAPHY

What matters about a place is the spirit of the land, the people, and the light. To rise above the visual trivia of postcard photography, the photographer must become sensitized to the specialness of a place and not fall prey to contrivances and preconceptions. Whether you are recording a personal trip to an exotic country or completing a travel assignment for a magazine or advertising agency, the photographs you make should be of events or people or landscapes that move *you*, not that you think may move others.

With the increase in people's visual sophistication, it is time for travel photographers especially to dump the organized platitudes of seeing and to make judgments of their own, to make photographs that are personal statements of moving experiences translated to film.

It is seldom easy to verbalize, let alone visualize, the feelings generated by a unique environment. I did not become sensitized to the soft, ethereal light of Ireland for some time. I was frustrated at first to see that photographs in the overcast light of the northern hemisphere looked either flat and dimensionless, with little separation of hues, or washed out and gray with no good blacks to add contrast. With experience I began to understand how to expose for proper saturation of the colors without losing highlights or destroying shadow detail. Many times neither the camera's light meter nor my Luna Pro were of much use in determining perfect exposure.

Each new light condition poses a new challenge and a new opportunity to the imaginative and flexible photographer. The camera is an immensely versatile instrument; the photographer is limited only by his or her imagination.

Note:
The technical notes at the back of this book will be of interest to nonphotographers as they contain anecdotes and personal insights about the taking of these photographs.

Come, heart, where hill is heaped
upon hill:
For there the mystical brotherhood
Of sun and moon and hollow and
wood
And river and stream work out their
will.

W. B. Yeats,
"Into the Twilight"

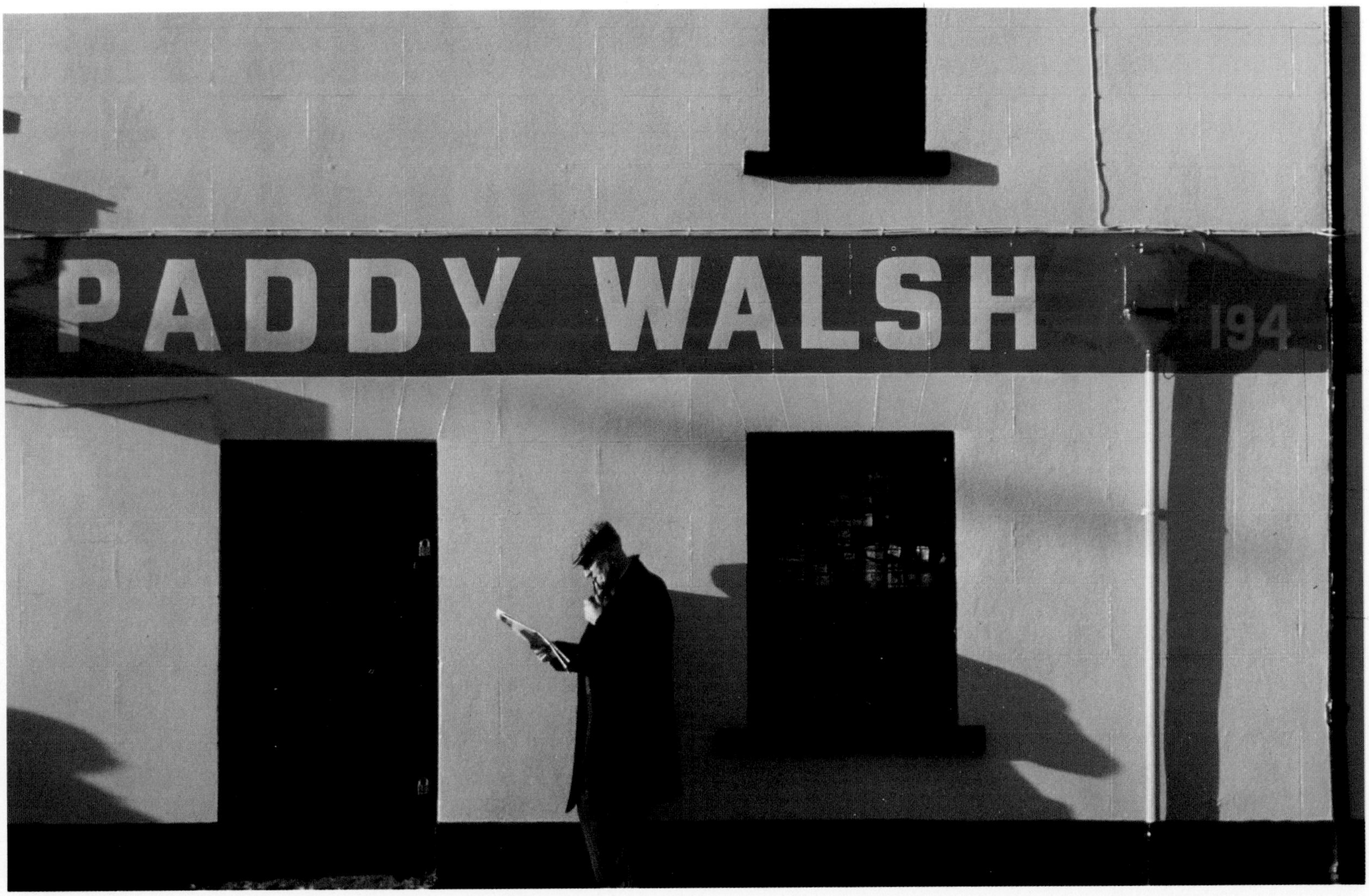
PADDY WALSH
194

Plate 3
Near St. James' Hospital, Dublin, County Dublin

Plate 4

South Circular Road, Dublin, County Dublin

MAJOR
VIRGINIA FILTER TIPPED
extra size
SRÁID AN MHUILINN
MILL STREET
POWER'S
WHISKEY
STOP
BAR
OLLY'S
SV

Plate 6

*News Vendor, Near St. Patrick's Cathedral,
Dublin, County Dublin*

Plate 7

Clontarf, Dublin, County Dublin

Plate 8

Irishtown, Dublin, County Dublin

Plate 11
Chimneypots, Ballsbridge, County Dublin

Plate 13
St. Stephen's Green, Dublin, County Dublin

Plate 15
Phoenix Park, Dublin, County Dublin

Plate 16

Stableman's Son,
Rathfarnham, County Dublin

Plate 17
Stableman,
Rathfarnham, County Dublin

Plate 18

*Christmas Day, Killiney Hill,
County Dublin*

Plate 19
Church at Clonmacnoise, County Offaly

Plate 21
Banagher, County Offaly

Plate 22

Alleyway, Banagher, County Offaly

Plate 23

Athlone Harbor, County Westmeath

Plate 24
Abbey–Leix, County Laoighis

Plate 27

Wicklow Hills, County Wicklow

Plate 28
Sally Gap, County Wicklow

Plate 31

*Master Glassblower, Waterford Glass
Factory, Waterford, County Waterford*

Plate 33

Near Skibbereen, County Cork

Plate 32

Mackroom Reservoir, County Cork

Plate 35
Lakes of Killarney, County Kerry

Plate 34
Ring of Kerry, County Kerry

Farmer, Near Gort, County Clare

Plate 37

Blacksmith, Muckross Abbey, County Clare

Plate 38

Cliffs of Moher, County Clare

Plate 40

Father and Son, Connemara, County Galway

Plate 41

Shannon, Lough Ree, County Roscommon

Plate 42

Blue Bells, Yeats Country,
Lough Gill, County Sligo

NOTES ON TECHNIQUE AND COLOR

Unlike many color photographers, I always prefer viewing prints rather than slides. In slides, almost imperceptible nuances of tone and hue are often washed out by the transmitted light of the projected image. The shadow areas of slides, for example, seldom retain the dark mystery so important to emotional impact (see Plate #31, for example). In good prints the reflected colors are saturated, never washed out, and the darker shades of blues or greens or red retain their subtlety and elusive beauty.

It is crucial for a color photographer to *previsualize* what he is seeing in three dimensions as a two-dimensional image, including what the impact of isolated colors will be. It should be clear how you want a color to *feel* or your exposure of the slide will be wrong, and it will be difficult or impossible to get a satisfying print. I have found that I consistently close down my aperture $\frac{1}{2}$ stop to a full stop from what the Nikon meter tells me (I don't like to rate the film faster, however, because I like to work with the full range of the indicated exposure reading between the plus and minus). I like rich, saturated colors, and even $\frac{1}{3}$ stop off will make life very hard for the printer. I'd rather be under than over, since I find I routinely discard slides that have washed-out colors and can often rescue slightly dark slides in the printing.

I nearly always shoot Kodachrome 64. The colors are splendid, especially warm tones of red and orange and yellow. The blues, while still being realistic, are richer and more intense than any slide film I know of, and even subtle pastel shades are beautifully rendered if the printer has the touch. Kodachrome 25 is too slow for the soft and late-afternoon light I prefer.

I always have a 4 x 5 inch internegative made of a slide I wish to print. The new Vericolor internegative film gives fine prints with the *c* process, and working from a 4 x 5 internegative gives the printer much more leeway in local controls. A slightly washed-out sky or a weak color cast in the foreground or background of a slide can be corrected by a skilled printer to achieve a more powerful, even if manipulated, pictorial effect. My concern is always with the recreation of the original emotional experience of the scene, and sometimes a drastic shift in the "normal" color balance of the print will achieve this equivalance (see Plate #25, for example).

Of course, if you are not a professional photographer and are primarily concerned with prints for your albums or walls, then shooting Kodacolor negatives, or especially Vericolor if you're careful about refrigeration, will give you beautiful prints. In fact, if you don't need slides for slide shows or art directors, color negatives will give you more latitude in the exposure range. If you are a professional photographer, it is necessary to satisfy the needs of art directors who prefer to work directly from transparencies. It is also easier to edit slides, and I oftentimes want to project a separately selected tray of slides to a prospective client.

For those who are seeking aperture and shutter speed information, I don't usually keep records unless I am testing the film or lens or experimenting with depth of field or speed (see the note opposite Plate #42, for example). I always keep my camera ready at $\frac{1}{125}$ (or $\frac{1}{60}$ if the light is low), and the aperture ring at f 8 or 5.6. This way I'm prepared for a scene change of one-second. I always

bracket my exposures if possible, in $\frac{1}{3}$-stop increments above and below the indicated meter reading. I have bracketed for a whole roll of film in some cases where I'm not sure what to expect from different versions of the color in the scene, and if I don't know how much shadow detail I want (see the note opposite Plate #38, for example).

I've used the same black-body Nikkormat for seven years without a bit of trouble, although I take with me a Luna Pro light meter with a spot attachment to get more accurate light readings if I need them. On my Nikkormat and my Nikon (one on my chest, the other over my shoulder), I always have a 35mm lens and a 105mm lens, the two I use most often. And I always have a 55mm Macro on my belt. I seldom feel the need for any other lenses, although I often take with me a 24 and 28, and a 200.

My primary advice about equipment is to concentrate on learning how you see, and then on shooting with the appropriate lens almost all the time. Then the camera and lens becomes automatic, and your vision is free to expand without gadgetry or tricks. The same thing applies for film; shoot one whose colors you love, and get to know its moods and latitudes, and then you'll learn exactly how to expose and print it for the emotional equivalents you are after.

Plate 1   I took this slide from my open car window with a 105mm lens. There wasn't a moment to waste. I knew that if the man moved at all I would lose the picture. His shadow was essential. Often a person will walk into a scene I am looking at through the camera, and suddenly the picture is there. This picture is one of the rare cases when someone was just waiting for me.

Plate 3   I knelt down and got real close to this child with the 55 lens. His hair was gorgeous, but he took off while I was switching to the 105. Now, however, I'm glad I didn't get any closer, because the dark wall is perfect for his Aran sweater.

Plate 2   A day's rain had been drying for only an hour, and the walls everywhere were still dripping. I had stopped at this scene before, since I lived nearby in Dublin, but something was always missing. The top part of the composition was dead. I walked over after the rain to see whether anything had happened to the wall and was delighted by the wet pattern at the top and around the window. (50mm lens)

Plate 4   This is one of those times when people walk (or in this case run) into a scene I am looking at through the camera—and make the picture. The low light made a faster shutter speed impossible, and I felt very lucky to have gotten this slide at $\frac{1}{60}$. Actually, I love the movement of the boy in back contrasted with the stability of the fruit stand. Of course, of the half-roll I shot, only this slide felt just right. (35mm lens)

Plate 5   So much that is Irish came together for me on this street corner: the green-gray wall, the Gaelic in the street sign, the ubiquitous Major's cigarette ad, and of course the whiskey sign and Molly's Bar. I aimed my Luna Pro (with 7.5° spot attachment) at the green wall in the center of the picture. I expected the direct sunlight on the bar door to wash out a little, but I wanted the wall to be perfect and I wanted to retain some detail in the shadows on the left top and bottom. I waited fifteen minutes for someone to walk out the door (someone finally entered), but I like it without the person. The picture feels more graphic this way, like the experience itself. (105mm lens)

Plate 6   It was difficult to expose this picture properly to get enough detail in the brightly lit part of the newspaper as well as a lot of detail in his face, so I shot ten or twelve frames. And I was standing in the middle of rush-hour traffic with my 105.

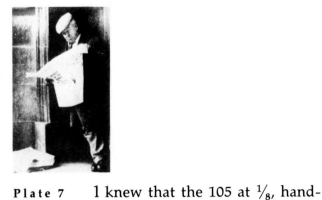

Plate 7   I knew that the 105 at $\frac{1}{8}$, hand-held, wide open, would not be sharp, but I held my breath and shot two frames because I felt he was about to move away (which he did). His eyes are closed in both frames, and for a while this was a reject slide. But now I feel it works even better with his eyes closed.

Plate 8   Pastel colors reflected on wet pavements are a great strength of Kodachrome 64! So is a saturated red like this door. A 35mm lens enabled me to surround the three bright colors I liked with darker space to set them off and allow them to play against each other.

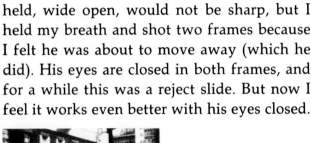

Plate 9   I could never resist a natural Mondrian! And red is always at its sexy best for me when it's isolated among grayer hues. The snow on the top of the wall and roof was the white the scene needed to come alive. (55mm lens)

Plate 10   I hoped the film would capture the subtle pink of the peeled paint (I bracketed by $\frac{1}{3}$ stops several exposures). The intense blue of the windowsill and side wall seemed to keep this Rorschach from flying away. (55mm lens)

Plate 11   The angle of the sun in this northern hemispheric light made for intense, fiery sunsets on three different occasions while I lived in Dublin. I took this from my bedroom window with a 200mm lens wedged into the windowsill corner to try and keep the chimney pots sharp. The light changed incredibly fast. The scene was gone in less than three minutes.

Plate 12   I love the pattern that twigs make when they're out of focus (although I hate "circles of confusion"!). (105 lens, probably at $\frac{1}{30}$, wide open)

Plate 13   This effect of sun through hazy light is something I always try to work with when I see it. This time I was lucky enough to get the right subject—a lovely tree. I bracketed a lot because I was unsure of how the sun would come out through the leaves. At f 8 with the 55, the diffraction pattern of the sun begins to show nicely.

Plate 14   I was struck by the symmetry of colors—the band of orange, the red freckles and hair, and the orange patch on the cap. I got as close as I could with the 105 wide open, hoping the background would be sufficiently out of focus.

Plate 15   The foreground area of this print was burned down quite a bit to keep attention on the light in the lower-middle of the scene. I shot at f 22 on a tripod, hoping the sun would star a little, caught between the branches of the trees (the "star" is actually related to the shape of the diaphragm).

Plate 16   I was so delighted by this scene in front of a barn fifteen miles from Dublin that I didn't even notice the red shirt the boy had on. When I finally noticed that red framed between the two red doors, I must have shot twenty-five frames in half a minute, chatting to the shy kid all the time. (55mm lens)

Plate 17   One of my favorite ways of making things stand out is to frame them against the blackness of a space like a barn or a doorway. I exposed carefully for his face and did not think about anything else. (55mm lens)

Plate 18   I could only hope that I would get the right silhouette of the walking man, his cane, and the two dogs. I hardly suspected the stick in the dog's mouth would show. This slide was a delightful surprise to me, although I shot a whole roll of the man walking toward the cloud. (105mm lens)

Plate 20   I wanted the two kids to be the only thing in focus in the picture, so I shot these frames wide open with a 105. There is a little circle of sharpness around them in the hay. I hoped for the three-dimensional effect that I was acutely aware of when making the picture in the barn. Her red dress floated in the space. I shot half a roll, bracketing for depth of field.

Plate 22   At first I struggled with a 35mm lens to get this amazing contrast of old and new, but I actually saw too much and the detail on the wall felt lost. The 55 was perfect, cutting the word "Lounge" at just the right place on top and bottom. I used a tripod and closed down as much as possible for maximum perspective.

Plate 19   Often a polarizing filter will do wonders for a pale blue sky. Here it also helped with the water behind the church, cutting the reflection. I exposed for the side of the church in shadow and bracketed five or six frames. (55mm lens)

Plate 21   I believe that composition is the bones, and color the flesh of fine color pictures. Color is a window into mood, but too often the initial impact of a color photograph dissipates for lack of form and strong composition. For me, subtle color, and especially monochromatic color, makes for the most fascinating photographs. (55mm lens)

Plate 23   Even a tripod didn't help in this low rainy light. The boat was floating around and unsharp in most of the slides taken at $\frac{1}{15}$ wide open. At the risk of losing the reflection of the blue color in the water, I took some at $\frac{1}{30}$ that were sharper. I did close down the 105 to f 5.6 so that the wall behind the boat would be passably sharp.

Plate 24   I chased these two apparitions around a wet field for two hours before they finally gave up on me as crazy but harmless (my technique was to run them, then change my position quickly and freeze). I wanted them behind those trees. Nothing else would do. This is the only time I have ever shot four rolls of film for one picture. But by the time they stopped in the right place, the light was so low I knew I would have no depth of field. I considered that less important than the possible blur of a moving horse at too slow a speed. I held my breath and shot ten frames at ¹⁄₃₀ and ¹⁄₆₀ wide open before they were gone. (200mm lens)

Plate 25   This is a case in which I had the cloud color intensified strongly in the printing. I wanted a slightly unreal look because the experience of seeing this particular sunset was extraordinary. The hill had to be as black as possible to get a good edge on it, so I kept bracketing on the dark side for two stops.

Plate 26   This picture was printed a little bluer than the scene actually was, because to me blue helps it look cold and lonely. I wanted the monochrome feeling to be in the print and blue also helped with that.

Plate 27   [March, 7:30 P.M.] Big shadows like this are hard to expose properly unless you get right in them to make a reading. I wanted enough detail to keep the shadow open, but I especially didn't want the light on the subtle green grass to wash out.

Plate 28   Exposure in fog, rain, and mist is a problem. A scene like this overexposed is terrible, without any good blacks to anchor the picture. But if it's too dark the quality of the light will disappear. I looked for a middle-gray area in the air above the stones from which to take a light reading. (35mm lens)

Plate 29   [February] Edge lighting has always been one of my favorite occurrences in nature, which is why I love to photograph the last few minutes before darkness on a sunny day. It's crucial not to overexpose a scene like this, or all the subtlety of contrast will be lost. I wanted just enough detail to see the color of the grass. (200mm lens)

Plate 30   These two old farmers live seventy-five miles from Dublin and have never been there! I took their picture with an SX-70 Polaroid first; they were in awe as they watched the picture develop. After that, they stood there for as long as I wanted.

Plate 31   The natural warm light of the molten glass was all I needed to take this at $\frac{1}{15}$ wide open with the 55 (f 3.5), but I shot a whole roll before I felt I had him sharp.

Plate 32   The 35mm lens opened up the space of this scene, and its excellent depth of field even in this low light after sunset saved the foreground and retained a sense of perspective. The color of the water was totally different at different ($\frac{1}{3}$-stop increment) exposures.

Plate 33   This light was my favorite for pictures in the open spaces of Ireland. The soft top lighting revealed wonderful textures and seemed to unify everything beneath it. The sheep's wool, streaked with dye to show ownership, was the color of the sky.

Plate 34   This shade of dark green is very hard to get and to keep from looking muddy in the print. I exposed for the highlights on the water, hoping to keep them fairly dark. I didn't care about detail in the rocks. (105mm lens, probably at f 16)

Plate 35   I aimed the camera's meter at an average part of the sky and bracketed. Then I aimed it at the lower part of the lake and bracketed for that. I hoped the mountains in the mist would come out as I saw them; they almost did. (35mm lens)

Plate 36   A 200mm lens was all I needed to keep from invading his space. He didn't seem to want me to come any closer.

Plate 37   I knew I wanted to concentrate on the complexion of this blacksmith, and the intensity of his face, so I asked him to stand directly in the light from the doorway to his shop. I exposed for detail in his face, knowing that the shadow detail would almost disappear. It took some study of two versions of the print to determine just how dark it should be. I wanted the picture to be mysterious like the man. (105mm lens)

Plate 38   I had a lot of trouble and some danger setting up my tripod in the right place to take this picture. I wanted the silhouette of the old man in the stone cliff, and I wanted faint detail in the grass, so I made a light reading for shadow detail with the Luna Pro, hoping the ancient watch tower would be misted but clearly visible. I bracketed exposures for nearly a full roll, some exposures ranging to over a minute. The sun had actually set already, but the ambient light was beautiful. (200mm lens)

Plate 39   I was shooting her husband way in the foreground, then grabbed the camera with the 200 and took this one frame of her over his shoulder before she objected strongly. Her blue cuff was a delightful surprise when I examined the slide.

Plate 40   This scene was automatically a picture for me. My only concern was where the dog would be—my attention was mostly on the two men and the road off to their left. I wanted some sky to keep the picture from being flat and to give the road a direction. I tried for as much depth of field as possible.

Plate 41   With the sun not behind a cloud the brightness range would have been impossible for the film to register, so I waited ten minutes for the cloud to come over the sun. (35mm lens)

Plate 42   Using a tripod for this scene was crucial, since I knew exactly the composition I wanted but needed to bracket the *f* stops to get the right depth of field. I shot two rolls of film of the scene, using a 35 and a 28 and exposing between *f* 4 and *f* 16. When I studied the slides, I immediately preferred the slide with the lesser depth of field, although *f* 4 was too shallow. The 5.6 depth seems just right to me, with a feeling of distance and softness around the trees and in the back section of bluebells. The eye focuses immediately on the sharper center and then moves out, much as it does in the actual experience of seeing these flowers in a woods.